Sun

Honor Head

QED Publishing

First published in the UK in 2006 by
QED Publishing
A Quarto Group company
226 City Road
London EC1V 2TT
www.qed-publishing.co.uk

A Catalogue record for this book is available from the British Library.

ISBN 978 1 84538 635 1

Written by Honor Head
Designed by Melissa Alaverdy
Consultant Terry Jennings
Editor Hannah Ray
Picture Researcher Joanne Forrest Smith
Illustrations Chris Davidson
Diagrams Chris Davidson and Jonathan Vipond

Publisher Steve Evans
Editorial Director Jean Coppendale
Art Director Zeta Davies

Printed and bound in China

Picture credits

Key: t = top, b = bottom, c = centre, l = left, r = right, FC = front cover

Alamy/Guillen Photography 13,
/Photo Resource Hawaii/David Schrichte 8-9, /Jack Sullivan 18;
Corbis/Tim Davis 4-5,
/Terry W Eggers 16-17, /Randy Faris 7b,
/Aaron Horowitz 5b, /Layne Kennedy 15t,
/Carl & Ann Purcell 10-11tc,
/Ariel Skelley 7t, /Chase Swift 6-7;
Getty Images/Elyse Lewin 19t, /Jonathan Skow FC,
/Leanna Rathkelly 16bc, /Stuart Redler 11b, /S Wilde 8b.

Words in **bold** can be found in the glossary on page 22.

Contents

Night and Day

The Sun is a huge ball of burning gases. It gives us light and warmth during the day. Even when clouds cover the sky, we still get the Sun's light. The time when the Sun goes down is called sunset. At night, when we cannot see the Sun, it is dark.

WARNING!
Never look straight at the Sun. It will damage your eyes.

Night and day happen because our planet, the Earth, is always spinning. It makes one complete spin every 24 hours. As it spins, one side of the Earth faces the Sun while the other side faces away. The side of the Earth facing the Sun has day while the side facing away has night.

daytime

Earth

Sun

night-time

The time when the sun appears in the morning is called sunrise.

Summer and Winter

As well as spinning, the Earth travels around the Sun. This is called its **orbit**. The Earth takes a year to orbit the Sun.

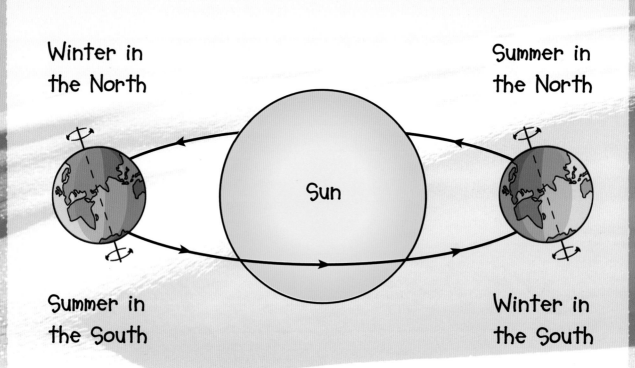

Winter in the North

Summer in the North

Sun

Summer in the South

Winter in the South

The Earth is tilted, which means it leans a little to one side. During its orbit, it is summer in the part of the Earth tilting towards the Sun and winter in the part of the Earth tilting away from the Sun.

In the summer, the Sun warms the Earth and it is much hotter. We can wear our summer clothes.

During the winter, the Sun is weak and has hardly any warmth. Now we need to wrap up warmly.

Hot and Cold

In the cooler parts of the world, the year is divided into four seasons: spring, summer, autumn and winter.

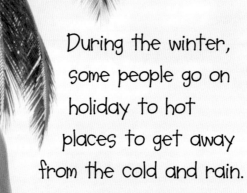

During the winter, some people go on holiday to hot places to get away from the cold and rain.

In places around the middle of the world, the Sun is hot all year round. In the Caribbean islands, such as Jamaica and Trinidad, they never have cold **weather** or snow.

In Australia, people can celebrate Christmas on the beach.

Different parts of the world have their summer at different times. In Australia, the hottest months are December, January and February. In other places, such as Great Britain, summer is during June, July and August.

9

In the Shadows

When the Sun shines, you can see shadows.

A shadow happens in a place where the sunlight cannot reach. A shadow shows the shape of the object that made it.

If you stand with your back to the Sun, there will be a shadow in front of you. This is because the light from the Sun can't go through you. It is always cooler in shadows because there is no sunlight.

As the Sun moves across the sky, shadows move like this:

Morning   Midday   Evening

A sundial shows the time. The marker makes a shadow on the clock face as the Sun moves round. Where the shadow falls, that is the time.

When it is hot, it is better to sit in the **shade** and stay cool.

Keeping Cool

If you get too hot you will feel ill, so your body has ways to keep you cool.

When we are very hot we sweat. This means drops of water come out through tiny holes in our skin, called pores. As the water dries on our skin, we feel cooler.

When it is hot we also feel thirsty. This is so that we drink more to replace the water we lose through sweating.

It is important to drink lots of water when the weather is hot.

Playing in water can help to cool you down on a hot day.

Animals in the Sun

When it is hot, animals need to keep cool as well.

Cats who have thick fur moult when it gets hot. This means that some of their fur falls out to make it less thick and warm.

If you have pets, make sure they have plenty of water to drink when it is hot.

Dogs pant to keep cool. They open their mouth, stick out their tongue and breathe quickly in and out.

Animals stand in the shade to keep cool on a sunny day.

Farmers keep their sheep cool by shearing them before the weather gets too hot. This means they cut off the animals' woolly coats. The sheep stay cool and the wool is knitted into clothes for us.

Helping Plants Grow

The Sun helps plants to grow. Without the Sun and rain, nothing would grow at all.

Bulbs and **seeds** in the ground start to grow when the soil is damp and the weather starts to get warmer. This usually happens in the spring.

In summer, fruits such as strawberries are ready to pick and eat.

During the summer, insects such as butterflies
and bees fly from flower to flower.

In the summer, the weather is even hotter. Flowers grow and fruit and vegetables begin to **ripen**. If there is too much sunshine and no rain, some plants die and the soil cracks open.

17

Fun in the Sun

The summertime is when most people like to go on holiday.

A trip to the seaside is the most popular holiday. People like to swim, play on the beach and visit interesting places. They might fly to another country or visit a beach in their own country.

The Sun can burn your skin. Always wear a sunhat and sun cream when you play in the sunshine.

On a warm day, it is fun to eat outdoors
at a barbecue or a picnic.

Camping is also a fun thing to do when the weather is
warm and sunny. There are many camping sites where
you live in a tent and sleep in a sleeping bag.

Have a Sun Party

Make Sun or seashell invitations

1. Cut out some squares of card, or use small paper plates.

2. Draw a Sun or seashell picture on the front.

3. Colour in and decorate with glitter or shiny shapes.

4. On the other side, write the date, time and address of the party.

Sunday
11.00
my place

Face painting

1. Buy some face paints. Draw a circle round your nose in light yellow.

2. Using dark yellow or red, draw triangle shapes to make a Sun face.

Have a sunhat competition

Ask your friends to each make a sunhat. Model them and decide whose is the best. Here's one idea:

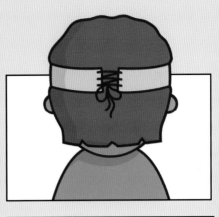

1. Make a headband. Cut out a strip of card that fits around your head. Punch holes at either end and thread with ribbon.

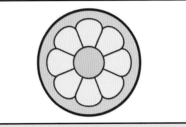

2. On a paper plate or piece of card draw a sunny picture, such as a sunflower.

3. Glue the drawing onto the headband. Tie on and smile!

Cool cubes

Make different ice cubes for cool drinks. Instead of water, put fruit juice in the ice trays. Try putting a small piece of fruit, such as half a strawberry or a raspberry in the ice trays, fill with water and freeze.

Glossary

bulbs   The swollen underground part of some plants, such as onions and tulips.

orbit   The path the Earth takes when it travels around the Sun.

ripen   When a fruit or vegetable has grown and it is ready for picking and eating.

seeds   Plants grow from seeds buried in the ground.

shade   A shadowy place where the Sun does not shine and it is cooler.

weather   The weather is what it's like outside, such as hot and sunny, wet and rainy or cold and snowy.

Index

Parents' and Teachers' Notes

- Look at the cover of the book. Talk about the picture on the front and the title of the book. What do the children think the book will be about? Are they looking forward to reading the book?

- Look through the book, showing the children the different parts of the book, such as the Contents, Glossary and Index. Talk about different kinds of illustrations such as diagrams and photographs. Which do the children prefer? What is their favourite picture and why? Look at the captions and explain their function.

- Talk generally about the Sun. What do the children associate with the Sun? (For example, holidays, heat, sunburn, sunglasses.)

- Talk about the need to stay safe in the Sun.

- First thing in the morning, go outside and draw around a child's feet with some chalk. Mark the end of the child's shadow with a small stone. Repeat this at intervals during the day. Discuss why the shadow moves.

- Have a competition to think of as many words with the word 'sun' in as possible.

- If the weather is good, organize a picnic. Go to the local park and talk about the difference between staying in the Sun and sitting in the shade.

- Ask the children to write a short story or poem about the summertime.

- If you can, grow a sunflower. Talk about why it is called a sunflower.

- Make a field of sunflowers. Ask the children to draw one sunflower each, all about the same height. Stick them on a blank bit of wall, or on a big piece of paper, to make a cheerful display.

- Keep a Sun diary on a chart on the wall. Draw squares for each day for four weeks. Let each child take turns to draw in a full Sun or half a Sun to keep a record of sunny days.

- Discuss why it is dangerous to look at the Sun.

- Ask the children to draw a sunset or sunrise.